FRANK LLOYD WRIGHT'S

UNITY TEMPLE

A GOOD-TIME PLACE REBORN

PATRICK F. CANNON

PHOTOGRAPHY BY JAMES CAULFIELD

UNITY TEMPLE RESTORATION FOUNDATION

FRANK LLOYD WRIGHT'S UNITY TEMPLE: A GOOD-TIME PLACE REBORN

Front cover: The coffered ceiling of the main auditorium of Unity Temple.

Rear cover: The decorative columns, cantilevered overhangs and lancet windows are signature design elements of Unity Temple.

Library of Congress Control Number: 2022905425

ISBN 978-0-578-39690-3

First Edition Revised
Includes bibliographical references.

Published by Unity Temple Restoration Foundation
875 Lake Street, Oak Park, Illinois 60301 708 260 6661
www.utrf.org info@utrf.org

This book was made possible by a grant from
the Richard H. Driehaus Foundation (www.driehausfoundation.org).

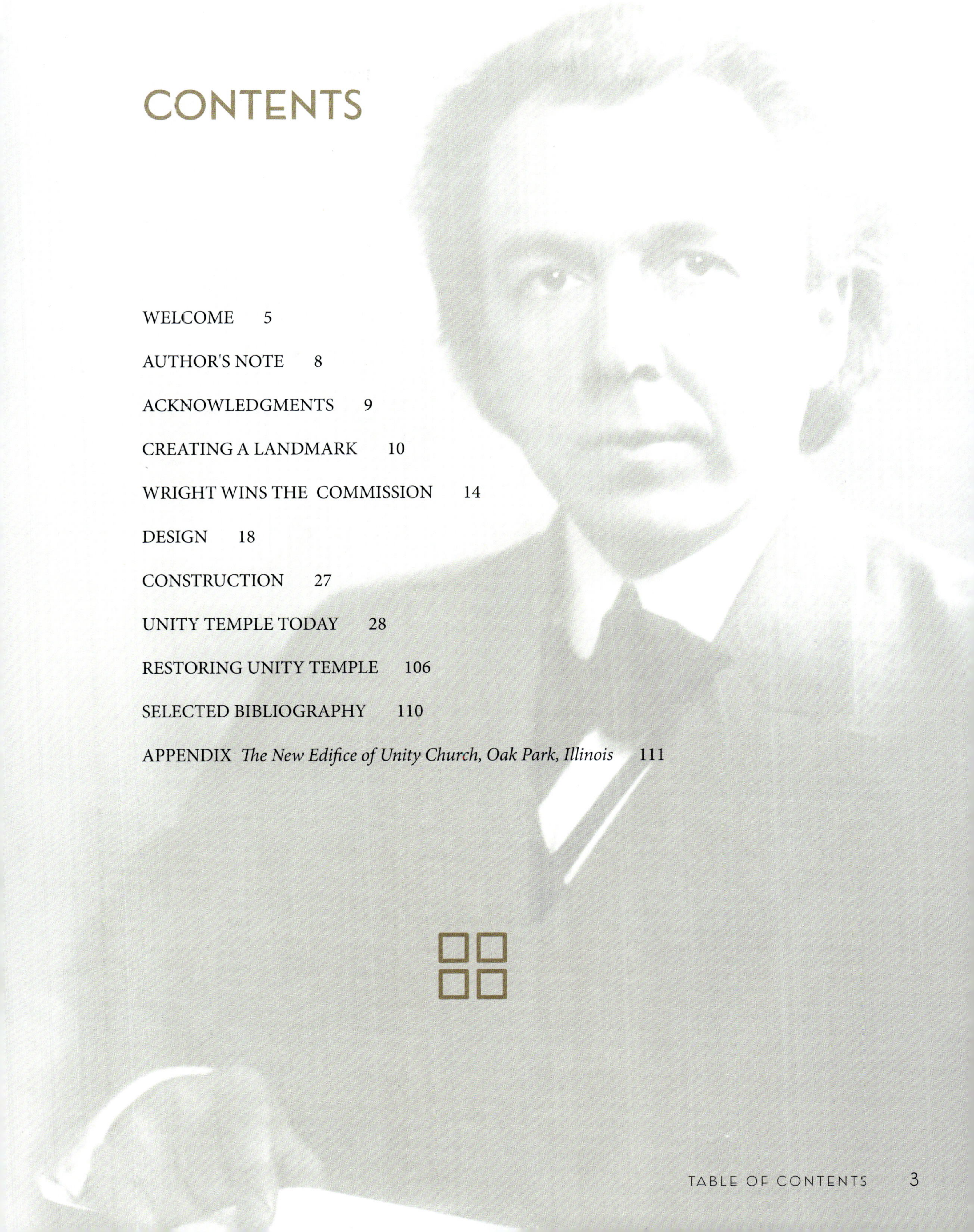

CONTENTS

HIP OF GOD
CE OF MAN

WELCOME

Why not, then, build a temple, not to God… but build a temple to man, appropriate to his uses as a meeting place, in which to study man himself for his God's sake? A modern meeting-house and ***a good-time place***.

— Frank Lloyd Wright
An Autobiography

Wright designed Unity Temple to lead the worshipper slowly but inexorably from the busy mundane life outside into the calm, boundless space of a "thought built" world within.

— Neil Levine
The Architecture of Frank Lloyd Wright

AUTHOR'S NOTE

In this book, the phrase "Unity Temple" will be used only in reference to the entire complex. Because it is shown as such on the plans, the part of the building that contains the main worship space will be termed the "auditorium". Likewise, the social and educational wing of the complex has always been called "Unity House", and this book will do the same. "Unity Church" will be used only when the original building that Unity Temple replaced is described.

ACKNOWLEDGMENTS

This is a revised edition of a book James Caulfield and I did in 2009, prior to the complete 2017 restoration of Unity Temple. Because of the restoration, we felt Wright's masterpiece deserved a fresh look, and this is the result. Aside from the historical images, all the photographs are new.

The book was made possible by a generous grant from the Richard H. Driehaus Foundation of Chicago, and its executive director, Anne Lazar. Jim and I have fond memories of being shown around his own home by the late Mr. Driehaus; it appears in another of our books, along with the Nickerson Mansion, now the Driehaus Museum. Born on Chicago's southwest side, he improved his native city in many many ways.

The Unity Temple Restoration Foundation (UTRF) has been our partner in this enterprise, and we would like to thank them and their executive director, Heidi Ruehle, who was with us every step of the way. For access to historical images, we are indebted to the Historical Society of Oak Park and River Forest, IL; Art Resource of New York for the Frank Lloyd Wright Foundation of Scottsdale, AZ; and the Frank Lloyd Wright Trust of Oak Park, IL.

For the original book, I had much help from friends and architects Jerry McManus and Jack Lesniak, both of whom at one time served on the UTRF board. The former minister, Alan Taylor, was also very helpful in giving us access to the 1906 brochure on the Temple, which is included as an appendix to this edition. Any errors, of course, are my responsibility alone.

Finally, I would like to thank restoration architect T. Gunny Harboe, F.A.I.A. for his thoughts about the Temple's restoration, which appear as a section in this book. His firm was not only responsible for the restoration of Unity Temple, but for many other landmarks, including Louis Sullivan's Carson, Pirie Scott store, now the Sullivan Center; and Wright's Robie House in Chicago, another World Heritage Site.

CREATING A LANDMARK

UNITY TEMPLE, still used today as originally intended, is widely acknowledged as one of the greatest works by America's greatest architect. Located in Oak Park, Illinois—Frank Lloyd Wright's own hometown for the first twenty years of his amazing career—it was a thoroughly modern building when it was completed in 1908, one that fully expressed the liberal religious philosophy of the Unitarians for whom it was built. Declared a National Historic Landmark in 1970 by the US Department of the Interior, it has also been designated as one of Frank Lloyd Wright's indispensable buildings by the American Institute of Architects; and was among eight Wright buildings named as World Heritage Sites by UNESCO in 2019. That same year, it received the Richard H. Driehaus Foundation National Preservation Award from the National Trust for Historic Preservation.

Now housing a Unitarian Universalist congregation, after the 1961 merger of the American Unitarian Association and the Universalist Church in America, it lacks overt religious symbolism, reflecting a rationality that rejects creeds, denies the divinity of historical figures like Jesus Christ while embracing their example, and seeks God as reflected in humanity below rather than in a heaven above. Thus, it is no accident that Wright's building has no steeple. As he more poetically puts it in his autobiography,

> I told the [building] committee a story. Did they not know the tale of the holy man who, yearning to see God, climbed up and up the highest mountain . . .? There, ragged and worn, he lifted up his eager perspiring face to heaven and called upon God. He heard a voice bidding him to get down . . . go back, go down there in the valley below where his people were—there only could he look upon God's countenance . . .

In Wright's view, a "church steeple, pointing on high" is "like the man who climbed on high" to see God— "a misleading symbol perhaps." Even today Unity Temple stands in stark contrast to its more traditional neighbors. Two Gothic churches and one Romanesque stood and continue to stand within one block of Unity, in a town once called "Saints' Rest" for the number and variety of its churches and its ban on liquor sales.

In addition to serving the religious, educational, and social needs of its congregation, Unity Temple has long been favored as a venue for musical performances and other community events. Musicians greatly admire its acoustics, as do their audiences. Speakers too appreciate it. The present author has given tours of the building and could speak to groups in the auditorium—even those in the farthest corners—in normal conversational tones.

But it is Unity Temple's groundbreaking exterior forms and inspiring, even transcendent, interior spaces that have made it one of the most important buildings of the twentieth century. It was begun as Wright celebrated his twentieth year as a practicing architect. In these two short decades, he had managed to create an entirely new and entirely American architecture. When the building was formally dedicated on September 26, 1909, its architect was weeks away from sailing to Europe to supervise the publication of a portfolio of his work in Berlin.

He traveled with his mistress, Mamah Cheney, causing great scandal when the liaison was discovered, and leading Wright to abandon his family and close the Oak Park studio. But the trip also broadened his architectural education, and the publication of the portfolio in 1910 introduced his work, including Unity Temple, to young European architects, who recognized that Wright had created a unique and modern architecture.

Frank Lloyd Wright turned forty while Unity Temple was under construction. By the time it was dedicated, in September 1909, he had begun to reinvent himself, and not for the last time.

Photograph c. 1904-1906, by an unknown photographer.

Collection of Frank Lloyd Wright Trust

Then, as now, three churches stood within one block of Unity Temple. Directly across the street was the First Congregational (now First United) Church by Edward Burling and Dankmar Adler (1873-1874). A block to the west and across the street from each other were the First Presbyterian Church (now Calvary Memorial) by William G. Williamson (1901-1902) and Grace Episcopal by John Sutcliffe (1901-1906). While each has its merits, the contrast with their new neighbor could not have been more striking.

Photographs courtesy the Historical Society of Oak Park and River Forest

WRIGHT WINS THE COMMISSION

Given his Unitarian background on his mother Anna's side of the family, it is hardly surprising—although not inevitable, as we shall see—that Frank Lloyd Wright would eventually be chosen as the architect for the building now known as Unity Temple. Wright's maternal uncle, Jenkin Lloyd Jones, was a nationally known Unitarian minister, who had helped the young architect get his first job with Joseph Lyman Silsbee. Silsbee had designed Jones's All Souls Church on Chicago's South Side, where Wright had married Catherine Tobin in 1889, and where he remained a member. But Wright was also sometimes listed as a member of Unity Church in Oak Park, where regular attendance would have been more convenient than traveling ten or more miles to All Souls.

In 1886 Silsbee had designed another church known as Unity Chapel on the Lloyd Jones family property near Spring Green, Wisconsin. Wright apparently had assisted Silsbee on the project, including doing a rendering of the modest building, which survives and is his earliest known finished drawing.

Lloyd Jones may have helped Wright's mother and his sister Maginel find temporary lodgings when they followed young Frank to the Chicago area in 1887. Their landlady was Augusta Chapin, pastor of Unity Church in Oak Park, and the first woman in America to have been awarded a doctor of divinity degree.

Appointed to Unity Church in 1886, Chapin remained pastor until 1892, when she was succeeded by Reverend Rodney F. Johonnot, who would remain through the years Unity Temple was being designed and built. Although it's unclear just how active Wright was at Unity Church, Johonnot would certainly have known him quite well by the time an architect was needed for a new building.

Almost from the time he was appointed, Johonnot had lobbied for a new building, feeling the original one, built in 1872 in a simplified Gothic style, was no longer adequate to the needs of a growing and dynamic congregation. A building fund was established in 1901, but a more serious fund-raising effort began in 1905. Then, on June 4 of that year, fate intervened in the form of a violent thunderstorm. Lightning struck Unity Church's steeple, setting a fire that ultimately consumed the entire building.

Almost immediately, committees on ways and means, site, plans, and building were formed. By August 1, 1905, the current site, at the corner of Lake Street and Kenilworth Avenue, had been chosen. The property was owned by church member and prominent Oak Parker Edwin O. Gale, who offered to sell it for $10,000, which was below market value for a 100-by-150-foot lot on Oak Park's main street.

The Wright connections begin with Gale, the senior member of a prominent Oak Park family. While working for Adler and Sullivan, Wright had designed two houses on Chicago Avenue for Gale's son Thomas, just a block from his own. Since Wright's contract with Adler and Sullivan prohibited him from producing work outside the firm, these two houses are among those often called the "bootleg" houses, which caused Sullivan, when he found out about them, to fire Wright in early 1893. Soon after, Wright designed a larger house for Thomas's older brother, Walter Gale, on the same block. All three were variations on the Queen Anne style, a legacy of Wright's time with Silsbee and the style the young architect had chosen for his own home.

Both the Gale sons were members of Unity Church, but Thomas and his wife, Laura, were also close personal friends of the Wrights. Later, Wright would design summer homes for them in Michigan and, in 1907, a new Oak Park home, which was not built until 1909 due to Thomas's untimely death. Designed at the same time as Unity Temple, the Laura Gale House is among Wright's best-known designs. Its cubelike forms are not unlike those of the temple. Both designs were widely admired in Europe when published in the so-called Wasmuth Portfolio in Berlin in 1910.

The original Unity Church was built in 1872 and destroyed by fire in June 1905. Its simplified Gothic style fit very comfortably in a community known as 'Saints' Rest'.

Photograph courtesy the Historical Society of Oak Park and River Forest

In his autobiography, Wright credits another friend, Charles E. Roberts, with being the most influential in his gaining the commission. Roberts was a member of the Unity Building Committee. Wright had done some remodeling work in the interior of Roberts's Daniel Burnham–designed home in 1896, and he designed several speculative housing projects for him that were never built. Also in 1896, Wright had designed a house for yet another Unity member, George W. Smith.

While these relationships were ultimately to prove decisive, the Plans Committee actually considered no fewer than nine architects before settling on Wright. Four of them, including Wright, were given serious consideration. William A. Otis and Normand S. Patton were both highly successful practitioners who typically designed in historical styles. Patton in particular had strong Oak Park connections. He lived in the village and had designed the Scoville Institute, the original home of the Oak Park Public Library, which was across the street from the lot upon which the new church would be built.

The other serious candidate was Dwight Perkins, a friend of Wright's, whose cousin Marion Mahony worked for Wright and later married fellow Wright assistant Walter Burley

Griffin. Also a Unitarian, Perkins was a member of All Souls Church and had actually collaborated with Wright on the design of the Abraham Lincoln Center, a multistory community center next to All Souls, for Jenkin Lloyd Jones. In the end, Perkins finished the building on his own after Wright was fired by his own uncle! To be just, it should be noted that Perkins himself was not happy with either Lloyd Jones or the final product.

In addition to holding progressive religious views, Perkins was known for his imaginative designs. In 1906 he was appointed chief architect of the Chicago public school system, for which he designed the deservedly famous Carl Schurz High School. Other notable public commissions included the Prairie-style Café Brauer on South Pond

The Laura Gale House (1909) was designed in 1907 for Thomas and Laura Gale, close friends of the Wrights and fellow members of Unity Church. It was built two years after Thomas's premature death.

in Chicago's Lincoln Park and the Lion House at the Lincoln Park Zoo, for which he was awarded the gold medal of the American Institute of Architects. He also designed Steinway Hall in downtown Chicago, whose many architect tenants included, for a time, Frank Lloyd Wright.

In his excellent 2008 study of Unity Temple, *The Noble Room*, David M. Sokol, professor of art history at the University of Illinois at Chicago, posits that Wright and Perkins received the most serious consideration for the commission because Reverend Johonnot felt strongly that the new building should reflect the liberal nature of Unitarian thought. Indeed, the pastor set forth his ideas about the building in a booklet called The New Edifice of Unity Church, Oak Park, Illinois, the text of which is included in the present book as an appendix. Johonnot does a much better job than the present author could of describing the religious thought behind the design of the new Unity Church.

Whether the final choice of Wright was made primarily by Johonnot alone or by Johonnot guided by Wright's friends and clients remains unknown. However it was made, Wright was asked to proceed with planning on September 16, 1905. The decision was made more public on December 17, when the Board of Trustees announced that initial plans had been submitted by Wright.

Clearly proud of his design for Unity Temple, Wright wrote a great deal more about it than he did about most other buildings. Much of what he wrote in his autobiography was an exercise in creative memory. For example, he claims that the church had contemplated having a design competition to choose their architect, but that he would never enter such a competition, which he felt led to mediocre buildings. While the church's leaders did not initiate a formal juried competition, they certainly had a group of contenders competing for the job. While Wright may not have known that as many as nine architects were initially considered, he almost certainly knew he was one of four finalists.

But however faulty Wright's memory may have been on this and other matters, one fact is certain: he got the commission, and the congregation got a masterpiece as a result.

DESIGN

When Wright was given the commission to design a new Unity church, it was with the understanding that its cost, not including the organ and furnishings other than the auditorium seating, would not exceed $40,000. In the end, Wright managed to spend nearly $80,000!

He was neither the first nor the last architect to greatly exceed his budget, which in retrospect (and in fairness to him) seems unrealistic even for 1906. The program, as it would now be called, specified an auditorium that would seat approximately four hundred people, classrooms, rooms for social events and utilities, a kitchen, a cloakroom, and a storage area. At first Wright contemplated using a steel-frame and brick-masonry curtain wall, as had been used for the recently completed Larkin Building in Buffalo (demolished in the 1950s). But he soon concluded that reinforced concrete offered the best chance of keeping costs within reason.

While the technique had been used for factories, warehouses, and other commercial structures, its use in a public building, particularly a church, would be groundbreaking. If the building were properly designed, the required forms could be moved and reused several times, thus saving both materials and time.

Although different materials were used, Unity would somewhat resemble the Larkin Building. In both, openings in the exterior walls were kept to a minimum to block out noise and other environmental factors. Light would come through skylights and high clerestory windows. Prominent corner piers would house staircases. Both buildings sat amid the bustle of modern life. The Larkin Building—the corporate headquarters for a mail-order business—was located in an industrial area adjacent to railroad tracks, while Unity would be on the busy corner of Lake Street and Kenilworth Avenue. Lake Street was the site of Oak Park's village hall, post office, public library, and several churches, as well as popular commercial strips to the east and west. In addition to the usual horse-drawn conveyances and quickly multiplying automobiles, it also had a streetcar line. And busy railroad tracks were only one block to the south.

Wright himself saw the two buildings as related. In his autobiography, he pairs them as revolutionary achievements. He called the Larkin Building "the first emphatic protestant in architecture." In the sense he used it, "protestant" designs would lead to a "reformation" in architecture. "Each new building," he wrote, "was a new experience. A different choice of materials and a different client would mean a different scheme altogether. Concrete was just then coming into use and Unity Temple at Oak Park became the first concrete monolith in the world. That is, the first total building designed for and completed in the wooden forms into which it was poured as concrete."

The preliminary design that Wright presented in December 1905 was substantially the one that was ultimately built, although he would tinker with details, particularly of the interior, almost to the end. "Thirty-four studies," he said, "were necessary to arrive at this concordance as it is now seen." At the suggestion of Charles Roberts, Wright produced a model to help the congregation better understand both the plan and the construction methods. It was approved on February 7, 1906. Working drawings were ready by April 28, and construction commenced in early May.

Designed just prior to Unity Temple, the Larkin Building in Buffalo, New York, shares its prominent corner piers, used for both stairs and air circulation. In both buildings, light comes largely from above. For the Larkin, Wright designed everything, he later wrote, "but the trash cans."

Wright's own studio (1898), just a few blocks north of Unity Temple, shares its bi-nuclear plan, with drafting room to the left of the lobby and the library to the right. Sculptor Richard Bock helped design the columns for both buildings.

Wright called the basic plan "bi-nuclear" ("nuclear" not having the sinister connotation it would later have). By this he meant that the building contained two main spaces, joined by a connecting entrance hall. One space is, of course, the auditorium; the other, which came to be known as Unity House, contains the congregation's social and educational areas. Although the dimensions are quite different, the Larkin Building is a precursor to this plan, but it is Wright's own Oak Park studio that is closest to it.

In his studio, built in 1898, the two structures are the large drafting room and the smaller library, connected by a lobby. Although the geometry chosen for the studio was the octagon, rather than the cube and rectangle of Unity, and the materials are entirely different, the basic idea is the same. Like Larkin and Unity, most of the natural light in the studio comes from above. Using this plan permitted the church entrances to be sheltered on the sides, one on Kenilworth Avenue and an identical one on the other (east) side, which originally faced a private home.

The form of the building was a culmination of both outside influences and ongoing trends in Wright's own work. Besides the Larkin Building and his own studio, other analogues can be found in house designs that included experiments with reinforced concrete. While the majority of these flat-roofed and cubelike houses were ultimately built with standard framing and stucco—like the Laura Gale House, for example—they certainly share a similar aesthetic.

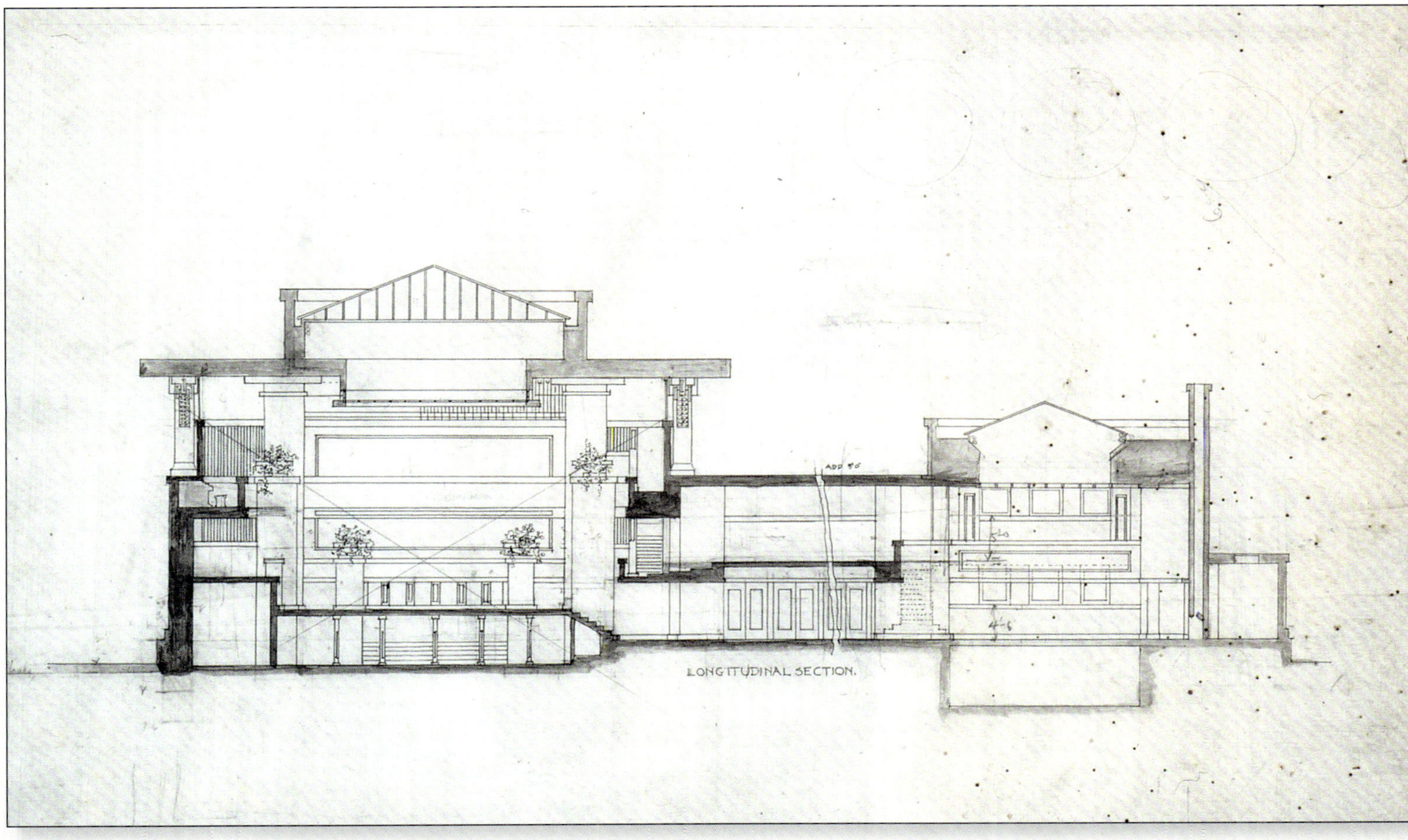

A longitudinal section from a 1906 drawing clearly expresses the building's bi-nuclear plan, but it varies from the final design in column and skylight details. © The Frank Lloyd Wright Foundation, AZ/Art Resource, NY

The Unity auditorium can be seen as a development of Wright's work on his uncle's Abraham Lincoln Center, whose auditorium Wright would later claim as his own despite having been fired before the design was finished. Moreover, while Wright was still with Adler and Sullivan, that firm had built the Kehilath Anshe Ma'ariv Synagogue (later the Pilgrim Baptist Church) in Chicago, of which only the shell remains after a 2007 fire. Wright may well have worked on it, as its square plan and auditorium closely resemble those of Unity.

Other observers have compared the building to Mayan temple forms, and still others have pointed out its similarity to the work of Austrian architect Joseph Maria Olbrich, particularly his 1898 Secession Building in Vienna. Wright was certainly familiar with Olbrich's work; indeed, he later wrote that Europeans had called him the "American Olbrich." Olbrich was Wright's exact contemporary (both born in 1867), but he died tragically young in 1908.

It is likely that these and other influences contributed to the design of Unity Temple and other Wright buildings. While he would have denied it, Wright was a genius at taking historical and contemporary influences and transforming them into something both better and entirely his own.

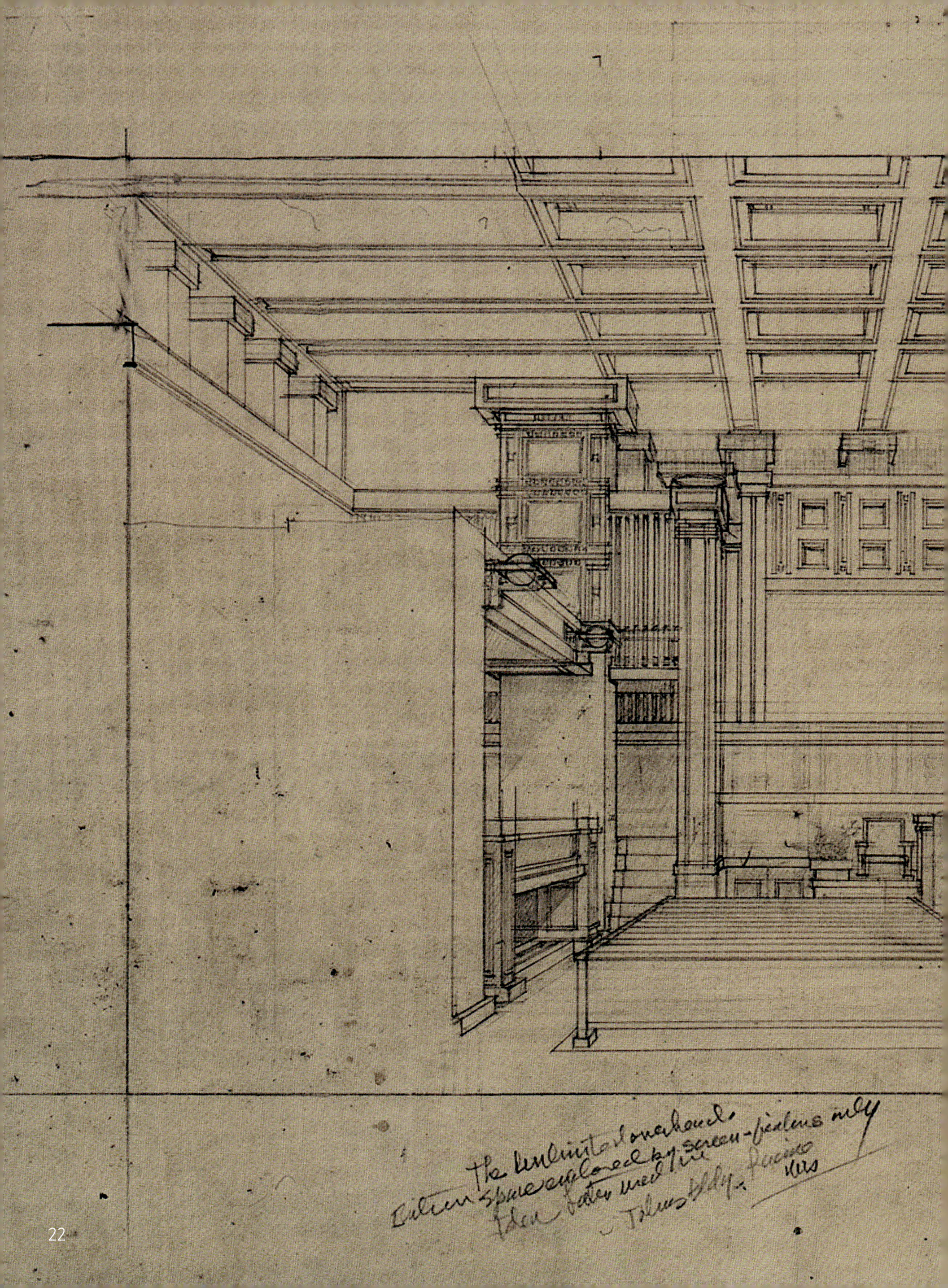

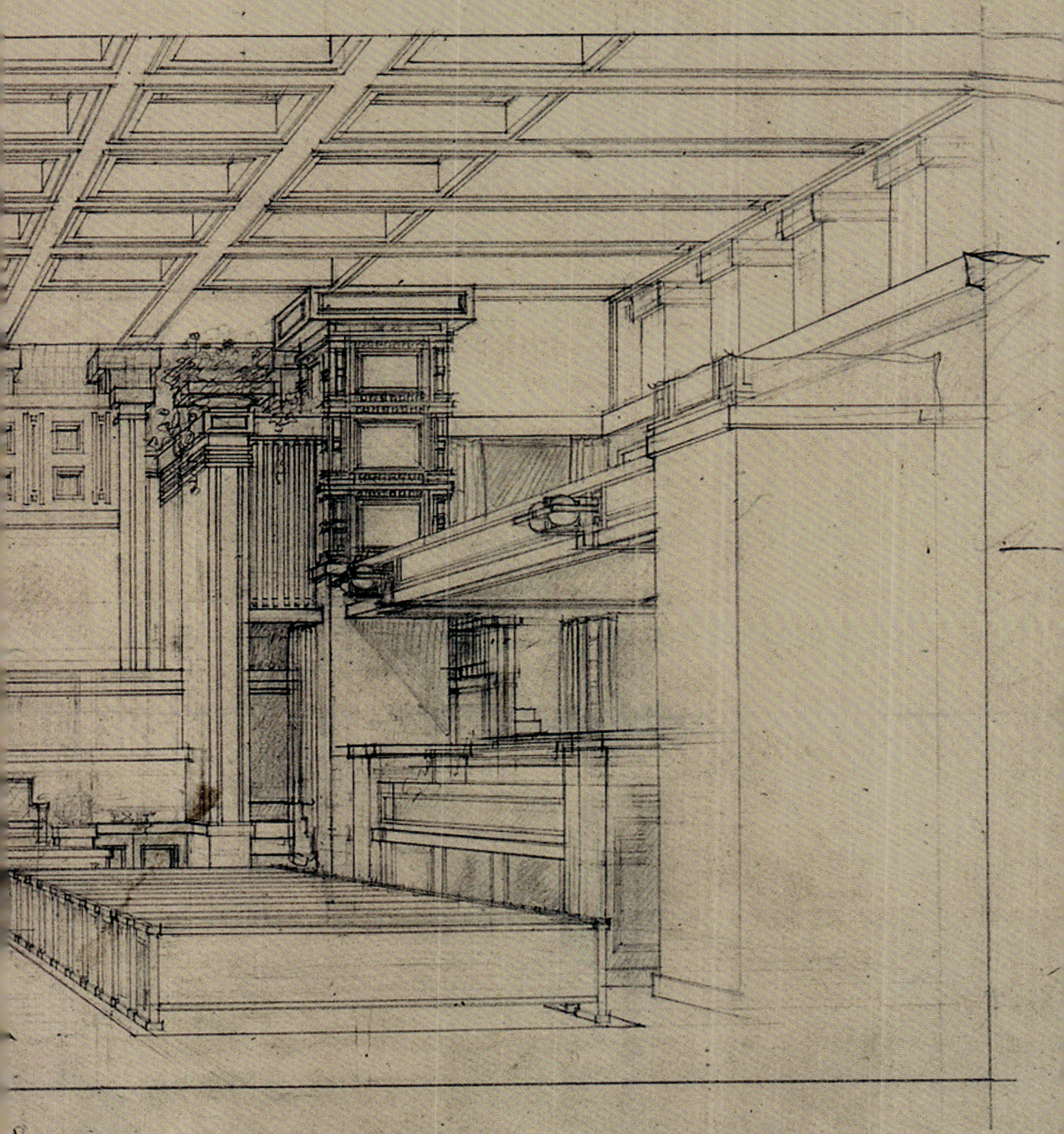

The perspective of the auditorium facing south toward the podium dates from March 1906 and shows a much more elaborate treatment of the main columns from the final design. Wright would refine these and other details constantly, often causing or taking advantage of construction delays.

A working drawing of the first-floor plan shows the footprints of the square auditorium wing and the wider rectangle of Unity House. Note that the balconies of Unity House, later enclosed, are open.

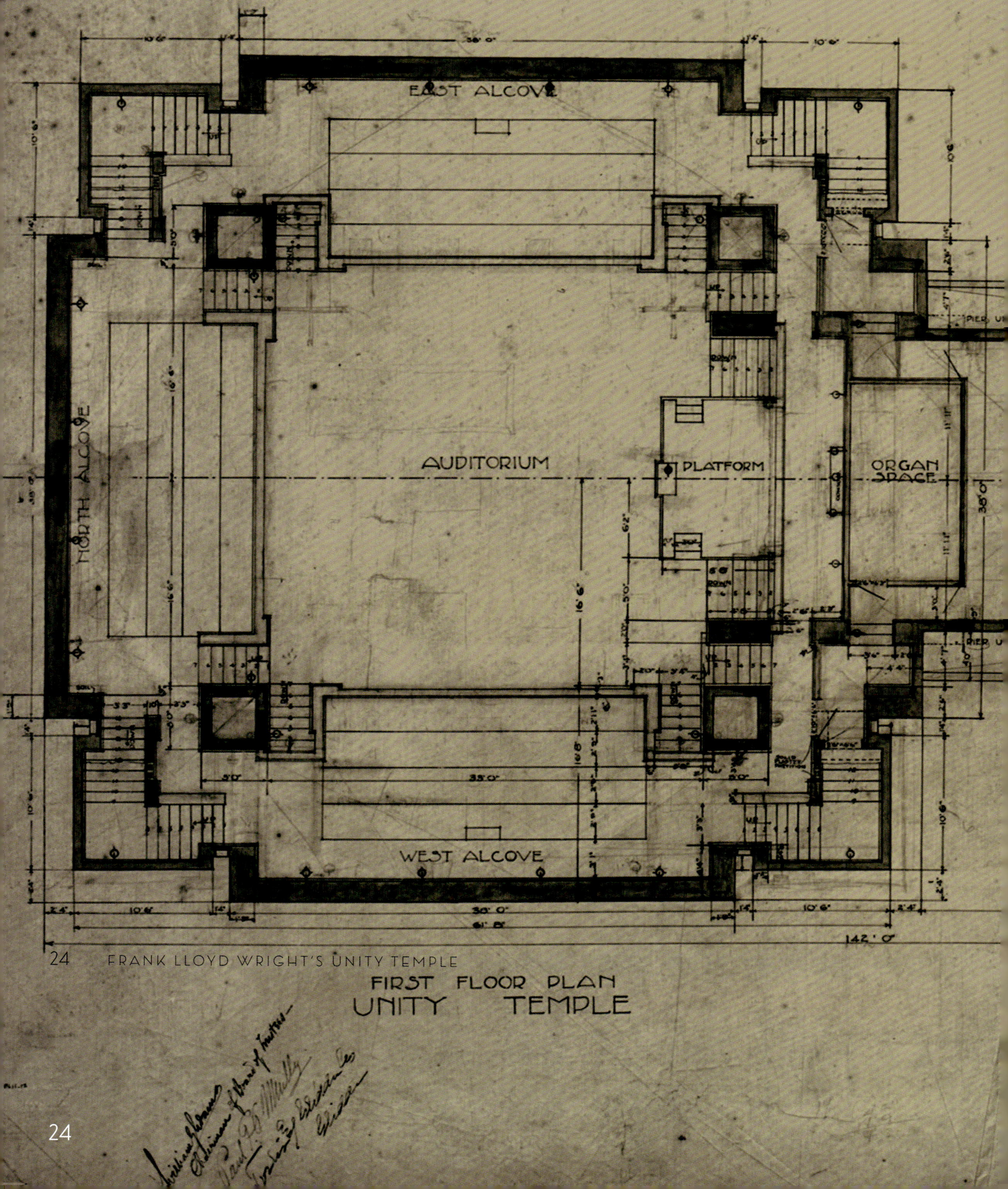

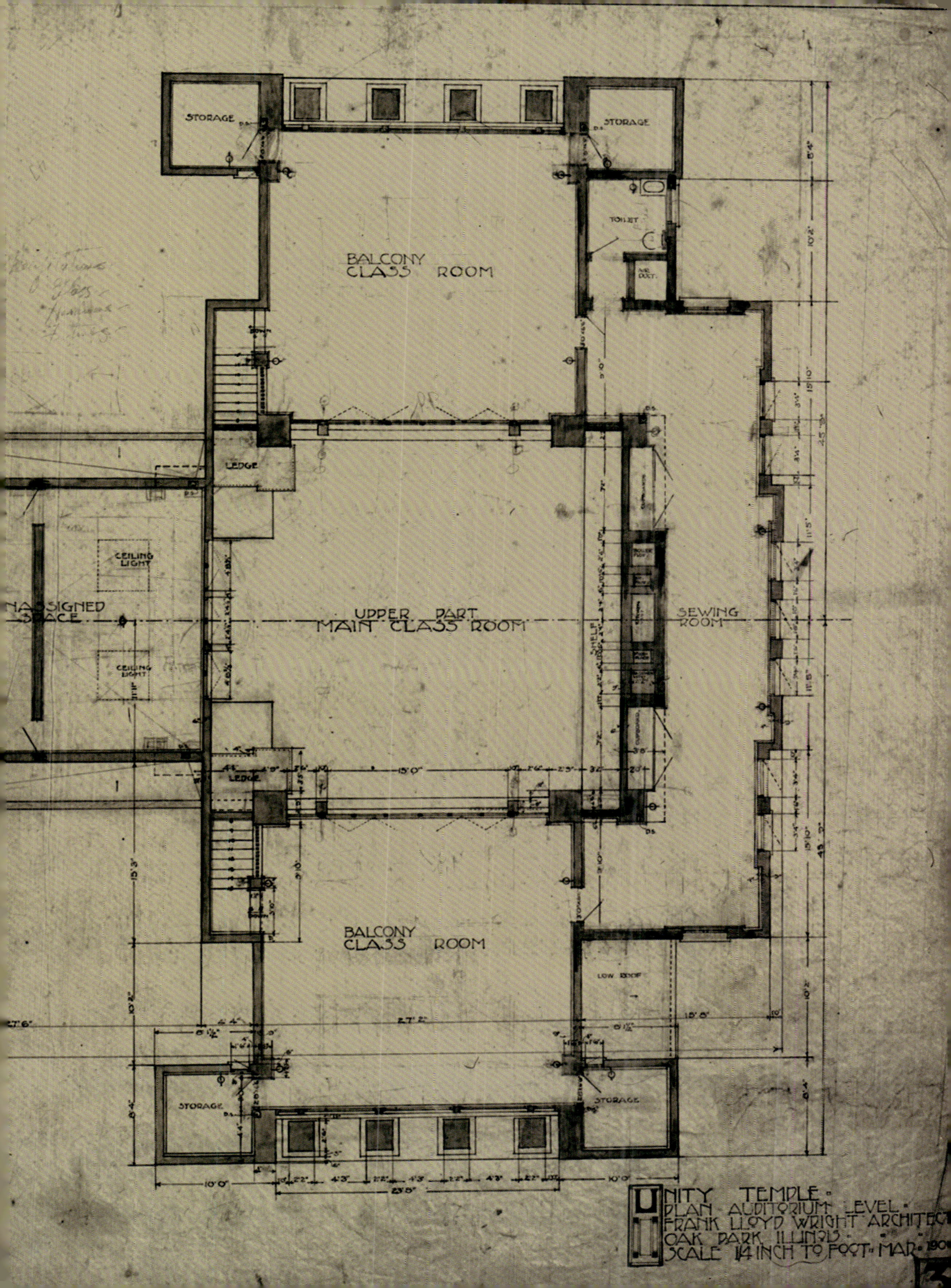
STORAGE
STORAGE
TOILET
BALCONY CLASS ROOM
LEDGE
CEILING LIGHT
NASSIGNED SPACE
UPPER PART MAIN CLASS ROOM
SEWING ROOM
SHELF
LEDGE
BALCONY CLASS ROOM
LOW ROOF
STORAGE
STORAGE
UNITY TEMPLE ·
PLAN AUDITORIUM LEVEL ·
FRANK LLOYD WRIGHT ARCHITEC
OAK PARK ILLINOIS ·
SCALE 1/4 INCH TO FOOT · MAR · 190

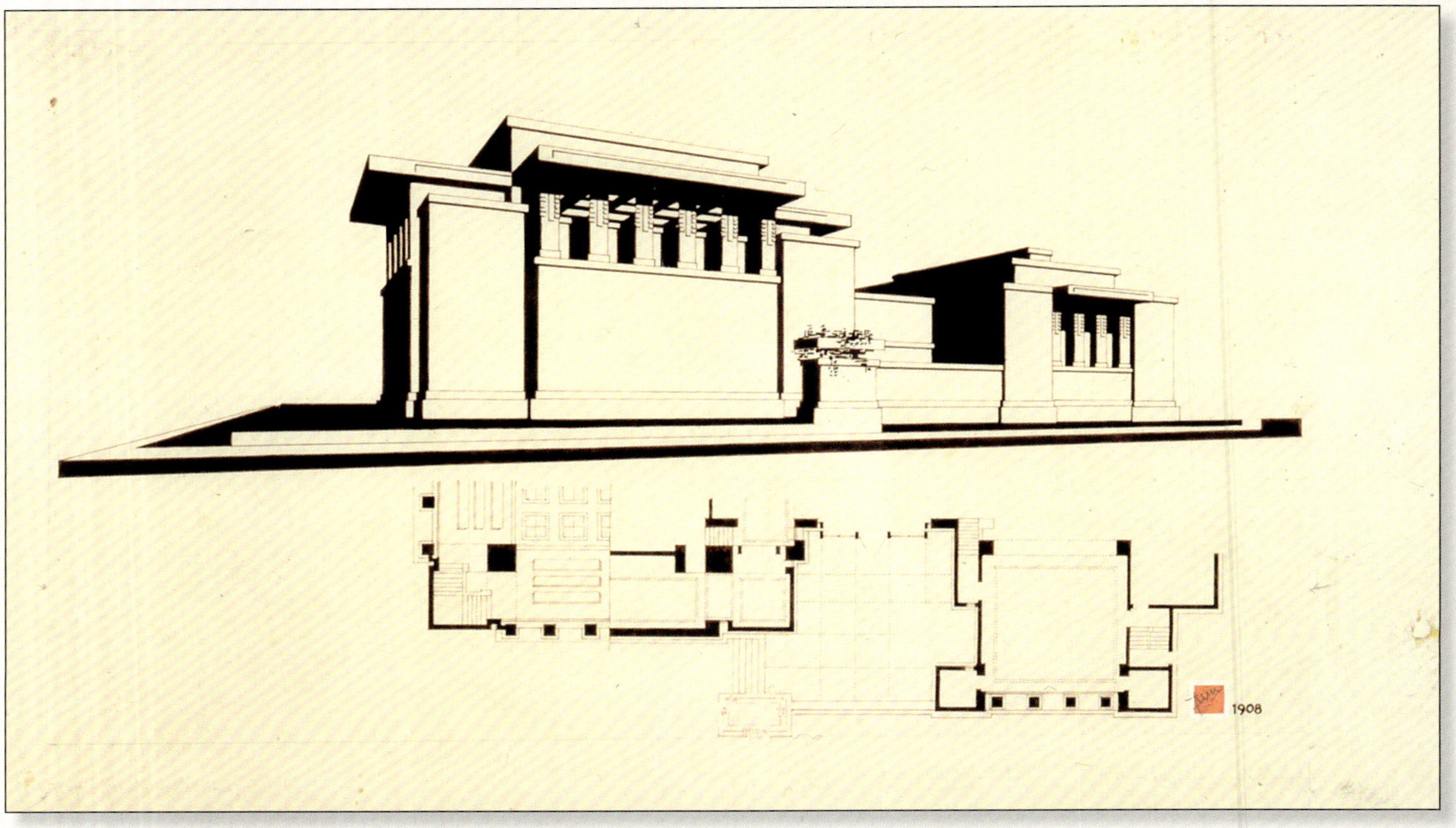

In this fascinating rendering, done in 1929 for exhibits at Princeton University and the Art Institute of Chicago, Wright seems bent on relating his design for Unity Temple directly to then current trends in European architecture, which have come to be known as the International Style.
© The Frank Lloyd Wright Foundation, AZ/Art Resource, NY

This photograph was taken shortly after the building was finished. Note the pour lines. During construction, the concrete was poured, then tamped down and permitted to cure before the next pour.
© The Frank Lloyd Wright Foundation, AZ/Art Resource, NY

CONSTRUCTION

Ground was broken for Unity Temple on May 15, 1906. The general contractor chosen was Paul Mueller, who had previously worked with Wright on the Larkin Building in Buffalo and the EZ Polish Factory in Chicago (the latter with a reinforced-concrete frame).

Mueller's bid totaled $32,221. Wright later wrote that Mueller "will build it for only a little over appropriation—and does it." We now know, of course, that the building costs continued to mount and would total nearly twice the original budget of $40,000. Although additions to the original contract were approved, Mueller was never able to recoup all his costs and was forced to declare bankruptcy after the building was completed. Wright does not mention this unpleasantness in his autobiography.

Wright's numerous changes and constant tinkering would not only add substantially to costs but also delay completion far beyond the originally hoped-for date of September 1906 (hoped for, that is, in 1905, before church leaders came to understand the length of time necessary to choose an architect and approve his plans). Even so, based on the plans as they existed in May 1906, Mueller hoped to finish basic construction before the onset of winter would—in those days—halt construction. (For a complete description of the construction techniques and Wright's design process and changes, see Joseph M. Siry's book, listed in the bibliography.)

Unity House was opened in 1907. While the auditorium was roofed by the onset of winter that year, it was not to be fully completed until shortly before the first service was held in October 1908. Wright was not responsible for all the delays. Funding problems caused some of them, Mueller having to stop work from time to time pending payments. Changes to the original design also caused delays and added expense. For example, Wright initially believed that only the piers and columns would require reinforcing rods, not the walls between. He later changed his mind, which added $4,000 to the cost.

Although it would take several years to finally pay all the bills, the congregation was happy with its new church. What many of the members had failed to understand and visualize from the plans became instantly apparent when they walked up the stairs from the cloisters to the auditorium for the first time. Here truly was, in Wright's words, "a temple to man." It was also a temple whose reputation as a modern masterwork was almost instantly established. To the amazement of the congregation, visitors soon began to arrive in great numbers, as they do to this day.

UNITY TEMPLE TODAY

WHILE UNITY TEMPLE TODAY is essentially the same building that Frank Lloyd Wright designed, several changes have been made, prompted either by necessary restorations or by efforts to make it more functional for the congregation.

The first change came almost immediately when serious problems developed with Wright's original ventilation system, which used fans to circulate heat from steam-fed coils through the floors to ducts in the columns and piers. This led the congregation to install a steam system with radiators. In 1961 the building exterior was resurfaced with materials that created a uniform surface instead of one that reflected concrete pour lines and form markings from the original construction. At the same time, the balconies in Unity House were partitioned to create closed classrooms.

Yet another resurfacing was undertaken in 1973–1974 to return the surface to a finish that more closely resembled the original, but still without the pour lines and other markings. A mix of concrete and pea gravel was sprayed on the exterior. When dry, it was lightly sandblasted to expose the aggregate.

By 1984 both Unity House and the auditorium had been repainted in the original colors, although not with the original techniques and finishes. Grayish yellow, yellow-green, and medium brown were the base colors used in Unity House, accented by dark brown, yellow-brown, and lime green. In the auditorium, surfaces like the baseboards and column bases were left unpainted, with other surfaces painted in pale yellow, pale green, and yellow-gray. To heighten the effect of entering the main spaces, the foyer was painted in a muted palette of gray and yellow.

Originally, the colors were applied in translucent layers of water-based paint over a white base coat and sealant, instead of the modern latex paints used in 1984. Beneath the original coatings was a sand-finished plaster that somewhat mimicked the exterior finish. As in the rest of the design, Wright took great care in choosing the colors to highlight and reinforce the abstract geometry of the decorative red oak trim.

Unfortunately Wright's choice of reinforced concrete and skylit ceilings had resulted in several periods of major restoration. The cantilevered overhangs, such a striking feature of the design, have been repaired several times, as has the necessarily complex roof.

Regular maintenance is carried out by the congregation. Since 1973, restoration has been the responsibility of the Unity Temple Restoration Foundation, which finally was able to close the building in April, 2015 and undertake, with a major grant from the Alphawood Foundation and additional support from the Tawani Foundation, a comprehensive restoration, completed in the Summer of 2017 at a cost of approximately $25 million. It was directed by T. Gunny Harboe (F.A.I.A.) of Harboe Architects, PC, which also directed the restoration of Wright's Prairie masterpiece, Chicago's Robie House; and his 1904 remodeling of the lobby of Burnham and Root's landmark Rookery Building.

All exterior and interior surfaces were painstakingly returned to Wright's original finishes and colors. All art glass was removed, repaired and conserved, as were light fixtures. Literally miles of Oak trim – for which the building is noted – were removed, repaired, refinished and re-installed. Electrical and mechanical systems were modernized, including the installation of a deep-well based geothermal heating and cooling system, which would provide air conditioning for the first time in the building's history.

To open up the balconies in Unity House visually, the partitions added in 1961 to create classrooms were removed and replaced by glass walls; built-in cabinets at their base are not visible from below, but provide welcome storage space. (For additional details on the restoration, see page 106.)

All of this work has returned Unity Temple as close as possible to Wright's original conception, while providing the congregation with beautiful and functional spaces for worship and community.

All the photographs of Unity Temple that follow were taken for this book and are arranged in a sequence similar to that experienced by a first-time visitor. If you have been to Unity Temple, these images should serve as a reminder of your visit; if you have not, they may perhaps encourage you to personally experience Wright's "modern meeting-house and good-time place." Information regarding tours is available on the web site of the Unity Temple Restoration Foundation (www.UTRF.org).

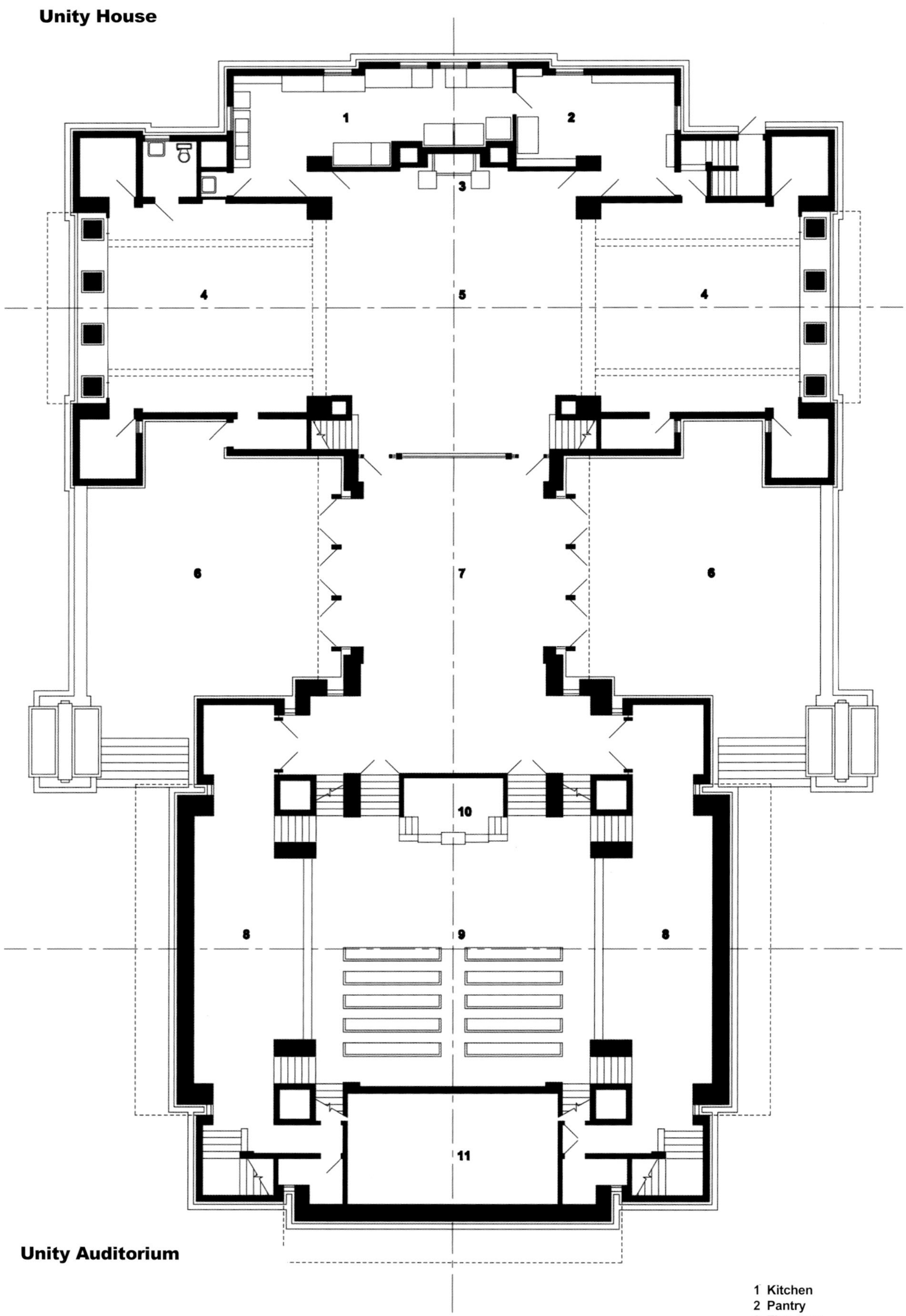

Auditorium Level

0 5 10 ft

0 1 2 3 m

North

1 Kitchen
2 Pantry
3 Fireplace
4 Office Space
5 Meeting Room
6 Entrance Terrace
7 Entrance Hall
8 Cloister Passage
9 Sanctuary
10 Pulpit
11 Classroom (Below)

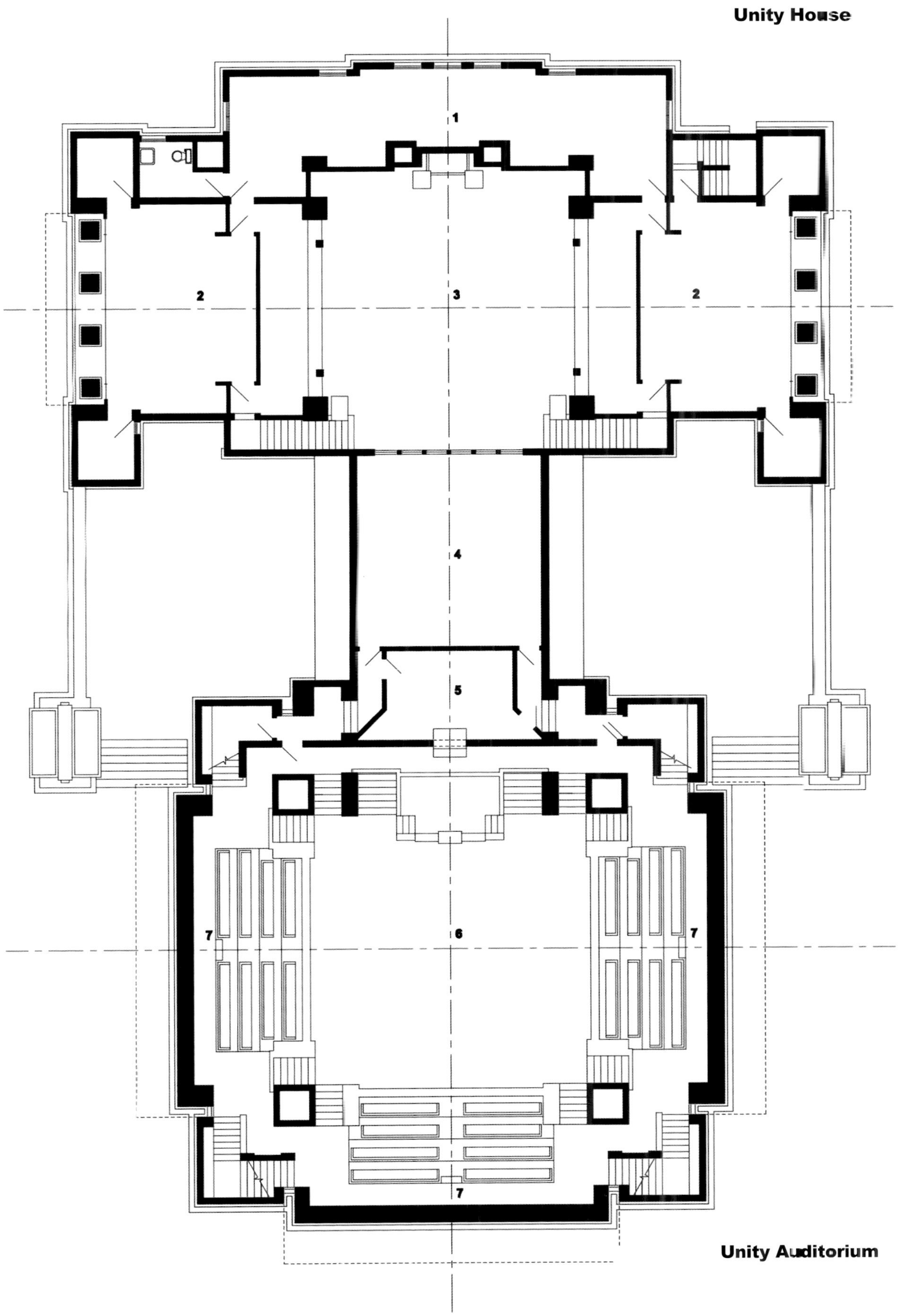

1 Multi-Purpose Space
2 Mezzanine Classroom
3 Open to Meeting Room
4 Pastor's Office
5 Organ Loft
6 Open to Sanctuary
7 Mezzanine Seating

Mezzanine Level

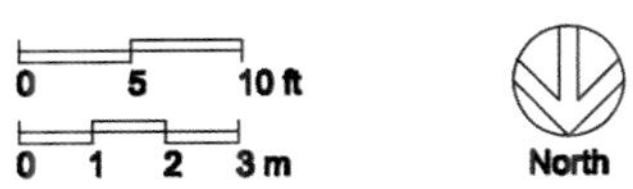

There are 32 of these columns in the building, all nearly identical. The design, executed by sculptor Richard Bock, is thought to be based on the Hollyhock flower. Wright often based his decorative elements on a conventionalization of natural forms.

As with the columns, the four corners of the auditorium structure are nearly identical, so the same concrete form could be used for all. Inside are stair towers that provide access to the auditorium's three levels.

ABOVE The west façade of Unity House, showing the clerestory windows.

FACING A private sidewalk leads to the entrance terrace, this on the west side. The massive planter – so typical of Wright – reflects the buildings overall theme of cubes and rectangles, as does the wall sconce.

Another view of the entrance area, this from the publ c sidewalk.

FOR THE WORSHIP OF GOD
AND THE SERVICE OF MAN

FACING The words above the entrance doors – identical on both east and west sides of the building – are in keeping with Unitarian principles. They are reproductions, the originals having been removed by vandals!

ABOVE This corner view shows the cantilevered overhang that's a feature of Unity Temple, and the lancet windows that provide natural light to the stair towers.

FACING This shows a full view of one of eight lancet windows. During the restoration, lights were in stalled at their base to illuminate them at night.

ABOVE Even these exterior sconces contribute to the "organic" theme of the building

This view of the entrance hall facing south to Unity House shows the low ceiling, muted colors, and simple light fixtures in this circulation space. Wright often used understated spaces like this to heighten the drama experienced when entering a building's main rooms.

In her biography of Wright, Meryle Secrest says that "the tenacity with which Wright clung to this device suggests that it satisfied his need to heighten the moment when, having threaded his way around all the obstacles in his path, the visitor would at last find himself in a marvelous, serene inner space bathed in light." The chairs and table seen here are reproductions, the originals having been sold by the congregation.

In Wright's view, every house needed a fireplace, and Unity House was no exception. There is a catering kitchen behind. Abundant light is provided by the skylights, which are protected by greenhouse structures above.

There are identical alcoves on either side of the main space. The light fixture globes are the only deviation from the cubes and rectangles of the rest of the building.

THIS PAGE There are balconies above the alcoves. Much of that space was later enclosed to provide classrooms. During restoration, they were opened visually by replacing the solid walls with glass.

FACING TOP These windows look into the space above the lobby, which served as an office for the minister. Access is from the auditorium.

FACING BOTTOM The stairs to the west balcony. The grill in the pier was a vent for the original heating system, which proved unworkable.

The east alcove. Note the radiators, which were installed to replace the original forced-air system. The occasional chairs are a form Wright used throughout the Prairie period.

This view of the northwest corner of the lobby shows the outside doors; the doors that lead to the so-called "cloisters" that provide access to the auditorium; and the exit doors from the auditorium. Shown open they have no handles on the lobby side.

This shows more of the outside doors and a more direct view of the doors to the cloisters. The southwest side is identical.

These views show the relationship of the cloister level to the auditorium.

Looking into the auditorium from the west cloister. This often is the first view a visitor might see.

This view from the east cloister shows the minister's podium. The pews were not designed by Wright, although they fit his scheme well.

"As in many of Wright's residential designs of the period, in Unity Temple one ascends from a darker low entrance into a bright ceremonial room. To go from Lake Street outside to a seat in Unity Temple's lower gallery, one makes no less than nine right-angled turns, as if the passage calls up the spatial experience of a labyrinth through different levels and conditions of light."

—**Joseph M. Siry**
Unity Temple: Frank Lloyd Wright and Architecture for Liberal Religion

"Space is the breath of art."

—**Frank Lloyd Wright**

During a sunny day, even the patterns of light from above seem to conform to Wright's geometry.

A view into one of the stair towers. The cube-shaped wall sconces are used throughout the building. The opening in the wall was once a vent for the original heating system; it has been repurposed for the new geothermal one.

A look from a lower balcony provides a closeup of Wright's trim scheme. Every piece of Oak trim was removed during restoration, refinished and reinstalled.

The auditorium ceiling has 25 coffers. The skylights are identical, although every other one is rotated. The light fixtures hang from the corner coffers, and reflect their shape. As in Unity House, only the globes offer a contrasting shape.

FACING The light fixtures seem to grow down from the corner coffers, almost like hanging plants.

ABOVE Detail of one of the light standards that flank the podium.

The cube shapes in the fixtures are a cirect reflection of the exterior of the auditorium; they even have an opening at the top that suggests the clerestory windows.

FACING It's interesting to compare the light fixture's form with the wall trim directly behind it. Note the three bands of trim on the ceiling; and the three boards used to support the fixture.

ABOVE The level above the podium contains the organ console and room for a small choir.

FACING Accessible from the cloisters, stairs lead to the upper and lower balconies.

ABOVE Lancet windows provide natural light to an otherwise dark area.

A corner of the lower balcony, showing stairs leading to the upper balcony. The lancet windows serve two levels.

5

FACING A section of a clerestory window showing two of the exterior columns.

ABOVE A lower balcony view showing (left) entrance to stair tower.

A view from the north to the east lower balcony.

The organ is on the next level up from the podium. Note the mirror. The grill once hid the organ's pipes, which were removed. The organ is now electronic.

A view from the north lower balcony shows two of the four main supporting columns. Wright spent a great deal of time working out the trim scheme. While certainly rectilinear, it seems more dynamic than rigid. Note how the column trim leaves the edges exposed. Two sets of stairs flank the podium, leading down to the exit doors and up to the podium and organ console.

There are clerestory windows on all four sides of the auditorium. Natural light is further amplified by the 25 skylights in the ceiling coffers. Because the light comes from above, the congregation is insulated from the noise and activity of the busy streets and railroad tracks that surround the Temple.

ABOVE The grill permits light and air to enter the stair towers from the auditorium.

FACING Looking north from the pulpit area.

Looking across to the west balconies.

Another view of the auditorium, this from the north upper balcony.

"The members of the Unity Church Society, in annual meeting assembled, desire to place on record their appreciation of the new church edifice.

The new building is a noble, dignified, beautiful and inspiring example of architecture and most admirably adapted to the various needs and activities of the church.

Because of its uniqueness in style and construction it is set apart as a thing by itself, at once honoring and distinguishing both its designer and its possessors.

Because of its simplicity, beauty and artistic effects it cannot but exert a refining and elevating influence upon all who frequent its portals."

Resolution of thanks by the Unity Temple congregation as quoted in David M. Sokol's *The Noble Room: The Inspired Conception and Tumultuous Creation of Frank Lloyd Wright's Unity Temple.*

GOD
MAN

WORSHIP OF GOD
SERVICE OF MAN

RESTORING UNITY TEMPLE

BY T. GUNNY HARBOE, FAIA

The restoration of Unity Temple took decades and required contributions from dozens of dedicated individuals, including members of the Unity Temple Unitarian Universalist Congregation and the Unity Temple Restoration Foundation (UTRF); architects, engineers, preservationists, and specialty contractors; and the talented tradespeople who completed the work. It was a great honor for me to lead the team.

Unity Temple is unquestionably one of Frank Lloyd Wright's greatest works and one that he often acknowledged as such. Its recent recognition as a UNESCO World Heritage Site, along with seven other Wright buildings, supports that claim. Unity Temple was chosen by Wright to be featured on the cover of the Wasmuth Portfolio of 1910, whose publication in Berlin influenced many young European architects of the day, including Mies van der Rohe and Walter Gropius.

The sanctuary of Unity Temple – Wright shows it as the "auditorium" on his plan – is a sacred space that will affect anyone who enters. Acoustically and visually, it is nearly perfect. On a sunny day, the room absolutely glows, and the surface texture and colors of the ceilings and walls are what make it so. But years of well-intentioned repairs and renovations led to a diminished experience for congregants and visitors. While still magnificent, it did not fully permit the experience that Wright intended.

The primary goal of the restoration was to return Unity Temple to Wright's original conception as closely as possible, while bringing its systems up to the current codes. The addition of a geothermal HVAC system now permits air conditioning to cool the interior for the first time. The restoration of the exterior concrete and new roof systems ensure that the newly-restored interiors will be protected from the water intrusion which had long plagued the building.

The restoration project was instigated by a significant event. In 2009, a large area of the ceiling slab near the podium gave way exposing the reinforcing rebar that had been slowly deteriorating, caused by a too-small drain that led to the subsequent failure of the adjacent roofing. Fortunately, it occurred during the night and no one was hurt, but something had to be done. Emergency repairs were completed, but it was now obvious that something more extensive was required.

The cantilevered overhangs had been previously rebuilt in 2000, which is when I first became involved in collaboration with the engineering firm CTL. The success of that project led to the creation of an overall Preservation Master Plan providing a road map for the full restoration of the building. It included a construction estimate of approximately $25 million.

Easier said than done! It was no small task as the congregation and the UTRF had been trying for many years to raise the necessary funds. The solution came in the form of an extremely generous lead gift of $10 million from the Alphawood Foundation. A substantial, multi-year donation from the Tawani Foundation, as well as donations from the congregation and UTRF supporters, along with a construction loan guaranteed by Alphawood for the remainder, meant that the project could finally proceed. Work began in April, 2015 and was completed by June, 2017.

The design and construction team was led by Harboe Architects, with Berglund Construction providing construction management support. Nearly a full year was spent in preparation, with research and mockups of the best techniques to execute the various aspects of the restoration. This included repairs to the exterior concrete as well as developing the proper treatments for all the interior surfaces. The extra time and effort was the key to ultimate success, saving both time and money in the long run.

The two most complicated elements were the proper mix for the exterior shotcrete (the spayed-on concrete, also known as gunite), and the sand-finished plaster and paint treatments for the interior surfaces. The original building had been constructed of poured-in-place concrete, with the exception of the decorative square columns at the top of the walls in front of the clerestory windows. Those were cast in four pieces in molds on-site, then erected and grouted permanently with more concrete. They were the only exterior elements that had not been recoated with new shotcrete during the restoration in the 1970s.

The challenge was to come up with mix formulas for the new shotcrete needed in all the locations where the existing material had cracked or delaminated, or was unsound and needed to be replaced. What made this so difficult was that when the work was done in the 70s, the contractors simply came up with an aggregate mix which was close to the original and applied the shotcrete in stages around the building. No special attention was paid to the fact that the cement used for the concrete may not have been a consistent color.

This condition was often encountered at corners where the repair work may have stopped and started.The new shotcrete contractor had to be able to adjust his mix accordingly. All the aggregates were determined but there was one particular pebble-sized flint aggregate that had been common in the 1970s yet there was now very difficult to find. Fortunately, a local material supply house specializes in locating hard to find sands and aggregates and the exact match was procured.

The rest of the process was managed extremely well, and in most cases it is very hard to discern the new patches from the 1970s work. However, there were several places that needed to be done more than once, and a few that were done several times and never quite matched exactly. It is anticipated that these few areas will continue to weather together with the adjacent existing material and with time will become a better match.

The other challenge was to replicate the interior plaster and paint surfaces. During this period of his career, Wright used a number of techniques employing sand-textured plaster with very thin paints to give his interior surfaces a soft and varied surface of great depth and beauty. The team experimented with a number of techniques to come up with the proper plaster mix, color application and treatments to replicate the original finishes. Our architectural conservators used microscopic analysis at 100 times magnification to determine the original colors and relative thickness of the paints as applied.

The freshly cured plaster itself was treated with an acidic material that allowed the sand to read clearly. This meant the sand aggregates were the critical part of the finish as the actual sand particles were a strong component of the visual texture seen in the result. It therefore had to be matched as closely as possible. Fortunately, the same company who supplied the shotcrete aggregates also located the proper sand mix for the plaster.

Once the plaster cured and the sand was exposed, a very thin custom mixed paint was applied to the plaster and then wiped off with rags to permit the paint to settle in the valleys and the sand grains to read properly. The results were then verified by our conservator in the lab. A large number of samples were created for each paint color and plaster texture to get the proper level of opacity. This iterative process was ultimately successful in achieving the wonderful glowing surfaces seen today, resulting in an amazing "organic" harmony that has not been experienced for many decades.

The other important components of the restoration included conservation and repair of the art glass, light fixtures, and wood trim. It all had to be carefully documented, removed to offsite locations, restored, and then brought back and reinstalled in its original locations. This involved dozens of talented artists and craftspeople who produced work of the highest quality.

I am proud to have been the leader of this team. Together we have returned one of the world's greatest architectural achievements as closely as we could to the conception of the genius who created it. I know you have enjoyed learning its history, and taking a visual tour of its glories.

Fortunately, no one was present when this section of the ceiling fell. But it did give new urgency to the restoration.

The Temple was completely wrapped to protect the local environment during exterior restoration.

Thorough testing of paint finishes saved time during restoration.

A plasterer uses test panels to recreate original finishes.

This worker is sandblasting shotcrete surface to reveal aggregate.

In some cases, simple repairs were all that were required.

SELECTED BIBLIOGRAPHY

All the books listed below have something important to say about Frank Lloyd Wright and Unity Temple, but the works on the building by Professors McCarter, Siry, and Sokol explore his magnificent achievement in greater detail. Each, in its own way, adds a serious and scholarly perspective to one of Wright's greatest buildings.

Brooks, H. Allen. The Prairie School: *Frank Lloyd Wright and His Midwest Contemporaries.* New York: W. W. Norton, 1972.

Condit, Carl W. *The Chicago School of Architecture: A History of Commercial and Public Building in the Chicago Area,* 1875–1925. Chicago: University of Chicago Press, 1964.

Gill, Brendan. *Many Masks: A Life of Frank Lloyd Wright.* New York: G. P. Putnam's Sons, 1987.

Hitchcock, Henry-Russell. *In the Nature of Materials: The Buildings of Frank Lloyd Wright,* 1887–1941. New York: Duell, Sloan and Pearce, 1942.

Levine, Neil. *The Architecture of Frank Lloyd Wright.* Princeton, NJ: Princeton University Press, 1996.

McCarter, Robert. *Frank Lloyd Wright.* London: Phaidon, 1997.

———. *Unity Temple: Frank Lloyd Wright.* Architecture in Detail series. London: Phaidon, 1997.

Secrest, Meryle. *Frank Lloyd Wright.* New York: Alfred A. Knopf, 1992.

Scott, Mark. Research Report, Unity Temple, Wright Plus 2017. Oak Park: Frank Lloyd Wright Trust, 2017.

Siry, Joseph M. *Unity Temple: Frank Lloyd Wright and Architecture for Liberal Religion.* New York: Cambridge University Press, 1996.

Sokol, David M. *The Noble Room: The Inspired Conception and Tumultuous Creation of Frank Lloyd Wright's Unity Temple.* Oak Park, IL: Top Five Books, 2008.

Wright, Frank Lloyd. *An Autobiography.* New York: Horizon Press, 1977. See also the reprint of the 1943 edition published by Pomegranate, 2005.

APPENDIX

TEXT OF BROCHURE PUBLISHED TO COMMEMORATE THE GROUND BREAKING FOR UNITY TEMPLE

THE NEW EDIFICE OF UNITY CHURCH, OAK PARK, ILLINOIS.
FRANK LLOYD WRIGHT, ARCHITECT, DESCRIPTIVE AND HISTORICAL MATTER
BY DR. RODNEY F. JOHONNOT, PASTOR.
PUBLISHED BY THE NEW UNITY CHURCH CLUB, JUNE, NINETEEN HUNDRED
AND SIX.

Every radical departure from the customary must make its appeal to reason to determine its worth and truth. Without good reason we should not depart from the customary. Especially is this true in regard to things sacred. But if the change is governed by sound reason, it compels an adjustment of thought.

In the new edifice designed for Unity Church [the original name of what is now Unity Temple Unitarian Universalist Congregation] by Frank Lloyd Wright, so striking an innovation has been made in church architecture as to make desirable a public description of the design and a statement of the reasons for its adoption, in order that its meaning and raison d'être may be more fully understood.

This brochure is divided into three sections:

DESCRIPTION
Commentary on Mr. Wright's philosophy of design

THE CONDITIONS DETERMINING THE DESIGN
Various conditions which existed and how the design deals with those conditions

THE EDIFICE EXPRESSIVE OF THE FAITH
How the building expresses the faith of this congregation.

DESCRIPTION

IN GENERAL

The fundamental principle of all architecture is that the form must fit the function; that is, a building must be adapted to the uses to which it is to be put and should express those uses in its form. A modern church building has a two-fold purpose; it is erected for the worship of God and for the service of man. These two functions demand a different architectural treatment that each may best be served. While a house of worship may properly be used for other services in the interest of human welfare, it is desirable that a religious society in building should keep its house of worship distinct from those rooms which are used for social service. By dedicating a place distinctively to worship an atmosphere can be given to it which is highly desirable.

In the design adopted for Unity Church there are two distinct buildings, one designed for public worship and other suitable meetings, and another for purposes of social service and religious meetings of a less formal character. They are, however, connected by a large Entrance Hall by which they are knitted together into a single integral and harmonious structure in outward appearance, thus giving unity to the two functions of the church, and guarding against the idea that the one purpose of worship is alone holy and the other common and unclean.

The name "Unity House" is given to the building used for social service, the name "Unity Temple" to the building used for public worship. While it is common among us to speak of our houses of worship as "churches," the use of the word "temple" is better for many reasons. It allows us to keep the word "church" to its distinctive meaning, namely, that of the body of Christian worshippers, and thus prevents much confusion resulting from the different meanings of the word. This usage also keeps us in line with the Biblical use of the terms; for in it the word "temple" is always used to designate a house of worship, while the word "church" always refers to the body of worshippers. The best lexicographers also recognize the fitness of this use of the word "temple," one of the definitions of the word in the Standard Dictionary being, "An edifice dedicated to Christian public worship." This building which is to be dedicated to the worship of the one true and living God in the spirit of Christian faith may then very properly be called a "temple." This term is further made specially fitting here because the building has the feeling and to some extent the form of an ancient temple.

IN DETAIL

The material used in construction will be concrete poured and tamped in forms in situ. The design is specially adapted to this form of construction and material and thus fulfills another fundamental principle of architecture.

The site of the building is a corner lot having a frontage of 100 feet on Lake Street, the main street of Oak Park, and a depth of 170 feet on Kenilworth Avenue.

The Temple is a cruciform building, 67 feet on each axis and 47 feet high. The form of the cross, however, is made less apparent externally, owing to the spaces between the arms being filled with square stair-chambers which rise nearly to the roof. The Temple stands in the center of the lot at the front. In the rear, with its main axis crossing the lot, is Unity House, 50 x 90 feet. These two buildings are knit together into one integral structure by a large Entrance Hall standing between the two buildings. The depth of the whole structure on its main axis running through the Entrance Hall is 143 feet. The two buildings are still further integrated by parapets extending forward from the ends of Unity House and enclosing in their broad arms the rear of the Temple and connected with it by wide flights of steps facing the main street.

Both the Temple and Unity House are lighted mainly from the top through large skylights shielded beneath by glass ceilings. A crown of windows also extends around the Temple beneath the broad projecting roof. Taking the light from above is an ideal method from practical purposes and it also embodies a fine religious idea. With the exception of narrow windows set deeply into recesses between the cruciform mass and the stair-chambers, the lower portion of the Temple is unbroken by doors or windows, save where it opens into the Entrance Hall. This preserves the mass of the building and by means of quiet surfaces and unbroken lines gives great dignity to the structure. This method of construction serves the further purpose of keeping out the noise of the street cars, thus securing a quiet and restful interior. At the height of 22 feet the wall of the Temple is recessed to carry columns extending to the roof, thus affording the necessary ornamentation and beauty to what would otherwise be a too severely simple facade. Behind these columns is a continuous sweep of windows. At a lower level the ends of Unity House are recessed and set with columns backed by windows in the same way.

Walls of shrubbery will extend from Lake Street on each side of the lot at its outer edges to the parapet leading from Unity House. Within these walls of shrubbery and extending past the Temple on both sides, walks will lead up to the broad steps rising two and one half feet to the large courts formed by the parapets and the adjacent walls of the buildings. From these courts on either side one passes into the Entrance Hall, 24 x 30 feet. Three sets of doors on each side, with a combined width of 30 feet, give hospitable welcome and abundant facilities for exit. This Entrance Hall affords an admirable opportunity for all the congregation to gather socially after service of worship.

Passing into Unity House from the Entrance Hall, one is faced by a large fire-place at the opposite side. Behind this fire-place is situated the kitchen with a large serving room at each end. The central portion of Unity House extends upward to the ceiling light, 17 feet, but at the ends the length of the room, 84 feet, is broken by galleries 25 feet deep. By means of folding partitions, class rooms are formed below the galleries or the whole lower floor may be thrown open for banquets and other purposes. Above the kitchen is a work-room for the ladies on the same level as the galleries and connecting with them so the whole upper floor can be used for social purpose without descending to the lower floor to pass from one gallery to the other. This upper floor is reached by stairways from the Entrance Hall, and also from the interior of Unity House. A rear door connects the kitchen with the street and gives entrance to the rooms for storage and heating purposes in the basement. Two toilet rooms and large closets are also provided.

To enter the Temple one passes from the Entrance Hall, at the right or left, into a cloister 13 feet wide from which flights of steps lead up to the nave four feet above. At the rear of the cloister, other steps lead up the alcoves surrounding the nave and to the galleries. Once within these cloisters, one is practically in the auditorium but is screened from observation by the raised floor and piers of the nave. They serve the purpose of sequestered aisles when entering the audience room. The outer sides of the main floor are raised four feet higher than the level of the nave over the cloisters and in the rear opposite the pulpit, making three alcoves separated from each other by the piers and stairways at the corners, and seating 54 persons each. This gives a clear view of the pulpit from the rear and sides of the room without the expedient of banking the floors. The level of the alcoves is reached by steps from the nave or directly from the cloisters by flights of stairs at the rear. These stairs are screened by large piers which carry the roof and support the floors of the alcoves and the galleries. These piers, four in number, one at each corner of the nave, also contain the ventilating and heating flues.

The choir is placed on the side next to the Entrance Hall in an alcove similar to those at the rear and sides of the nave, and on a level with them. These four alcoves form the arms of a Greek cross. The organ is directly behind the choir, but on a higher level, while the pulpit-platform is in front of the choir and separated from it by a high rail and at a lower level, projecting into the nave. Behind the organ are rooms for the choir, trustees and pastor's study, which are reached from the choir-alcove. They form the second story of the Entrance Hall. A gallery is carried around the three sides of the nave above the alcoves but is cut away on the fourth side above the choir to give room for the organ.

This provides accommodations for 153 sittings when needed. A total capacity of 450 is thus obtained, while a smaller audience can be seated on the main floor without the appearance of an empty church. The front of the gallery being carried on the large corner piers, these form the boundary lines of the nave. By recessing the gallery in this way, the ordinary unsightly projection into the nave is obviated and gallery made to form an integral part of the construction.

An interesting feature of the interior arrangement is that the congregation in passing out, at the close of services, moves toward the altar instead of away from it, thus contributing a fine religious conception and also adding to the social function of the service by making it easy for pastor and officers to meet all members and strangers without effort. Additional exits for this purpose are provided by wide steps leading past the pulpit into the Entrance Hall. These stairways are closed by outer doors and will not be used for entrance at times of regular services; but they may be used when desired as upon occasions of funerals, when the casket can be brought before the altar and taken out without being carried through the aisles.

Below the main floor is a cloak room, 31 feet square, which opens into the Entrance Hall, and is provided with toilet rooms in the rear.

While this edifice is a wide departure from the ordinary forms for church architecture, both in interior arrangement and exterior appearance, the design is simple, truthful, dignified and reverent in feeling and the plan is finely adapted to the work of the church.

THE CONDITIONS DETERMINING THE DESIGN

The plan and style of architecture have been determined by no desire to create something unique, but are founded upon substantial reasons; they are the natural and even necessary outcome of existing conditions, the rational solution of a given problem.

THE CONDITIONS OF THE PROBLEM

These consisted in the limited financial resources of the society; the nature of the location and environment; and the desire to express in the form and nature of the structure the faith held by the congregation erecting it.

The financial resources of the congregation limited it to a building costing not more than $40,000. The location on the main street of the village in the midst of a group of many fine public buildings, none of which cost less than $65,000, and others from $75,000 to $100,000, imposed the civic obligation of creating a building worthy of its environment. Several of these edifices are churches forcing a competition in kind. In the front and rear are several car lines whose noise must be shut out.

These conditions created a most difficult problem. It could not be solved upon the lines of traditional and customary church architecture, since a building of the same kind as those surrounding it, but cheaper, would suffer by comparison. A direct entrance would also let in the noise.

HOW THE PROBLEM WAS SOLVED

The skill of the architect has been shown by the successful meeting of these conditions. First, by the use of concrete poured and tamped in forms as a building material; second, by a design perfectly adapted to this kind of construction; third, by the adoption of a new and distinct style of architecture; fourth, by the method of approach and entrance.

Concrete is much less expensive than stone, yet treated in this way gives an equally dignified and substantial structure. Walls, floors and roof will be built out of it, thus involving little skilled labor and the employment mainly of but one set of workmen. This construction also gives a building absolutely fireproof. The style of architecture eliminates the cost of spire, tower, and expensive roof and lends itself to the material and construction used. Thus the problem of a dignified and substantial building at a comparatively small cost is met.

By adopting a distinct and characteristic style of architecture the building stands on its own merits and frees itself from any depreciatory contrasts with other costlier churches. The beauty of the classic design meets the civic obligation imposed by the location and environment. The style of the architecture gives a religious effect, expressing faith, aspiration and reverence without the adjuncts of a spire, tower, or soaring roof, which are commonly used to express these sentiments. The problem arising from the noise of the street cars has been solved, and a quiet restful interior insured by carrying the entrance away from the street-front and by keeping the lower walls at the exposed front and side unbroken by doors or windows, the light being taken from the top.

The religious feeling which every house of worship should express has been reached in this structure no by the adoption of the traditional form of architecture to which we are accustomed, springing out of the Gothic style of the Middle Ages, but by a frank return to the simpler and more ancient forms of religious architecture.

By the simplicity and beauty of the design and by its departure from traditional lines, the simplicity and freedom of the faith held by the members of Unity Church is outwardly expressed; the architecture thus typifies the faith of the church.

By these means every condition has been successfully met and the difficult problem confronting the architect truthfully solved. The society secures a building at an expense within its resources, ample in size, an ornament to the village, religious in feeling, fitted to the uses and work of the church, and typical of its characteristic spirit of simple faith and freedom.

THE EDIFICE EXPRESSIVE OF THE FAITH

Mr. De Kay has raised the question whether a church edifice ought not to express the special faith of those who worship in it. This thought certainly lies in line with the fundamental principle of church architecture. He says, "Perhaps we are on the threshold of a new era in ecclesiastical architecture, when one congregation will not copy another as one man copies another's coat, but the architect will be asked to say something to the point which cannot be misunderstood by believers."

This thought has entered into the architecture of this edifice. The attempt has been made not merely to create a religious structure, but one that fitly embodies the principles of liberal religion for which this church stands.

These principles may be said to be unity, truth, beauty, simplicity, freedom and reason.

UNITY

The building is a harmonious unit, the style fitting the material and the material the form. While the structure is adapted to the various functions of the church, the purpose of worship and service are clearly integrated, while separately set forth.

Informed by the same spirit which characterized the ancient temple, this structure typifies the thought that "while religions are many, religion is one," and that the vital power and superiority of Unitarian Universalism consists in its ability to absorb, perfect, and use whatever was good in all preceding forms of religion. The past and the present forms of religion are thus brought together in a spirit of unity. The temple form is especially fitted to a liberal church whose faith is that all religions are of God, are the attempts of man to feel after and find Him "in whom we live and move and have our being."

TRUTH

By fitting the organic nature of the design to the material of which it is built, by using the same material in every wall of the building, making the rear as good as the front and the whole logically consistent, the edifice stands for loyalty to truth. By the durable character of this adamantine concrete, used in this direct way, it also typifies the permanence of truth. It is honest to all its construction.

SIMPLICITY AND BEAUTY

The basic faith of Unity Church is that God is our good father who, by his love and his power, will bring all his children unto holiness and happiness. The simplicity and beauty of this faith are fittingly embodied in the simple design and chaste beauty of its edifice.

REASON AND FREEDOM

Liberal religion stands for freedom from the traditional, when tradition is not supported by good reason. Not blind authority but open-eyed truth and reason must control our creeds and our deeds. By cutting free from the customary forms in order to solve a difficult architectural problem, by adopting a design based wholly upon what is reasonable and fitting under existing conditions, the church has expressed its faith in the very form of its edifice. The building is an example of freedom based upon reason. It is an embodiment of the rational position that the vital question about a church edifice is not, does it look like other church buildings? but rather, is it genuine, is it rational? Is it true to the conditions? Its religious character is to be tested not by its resemblances to other churches, but by its possession of the qualities of reverence, dignity, and aspiration which belong to a house of worship.

These qualities are present in this edifice in a marked degree. Without tower or spire it expresses the spirit of the ideal. By its form it expresses the thought, inherent in the liberal faith, that God should not be sought in the sky, but on earth among the children of men. His word is not in the heavens that we should say, "Who shall go up for us to heaven and bring it unto us that we may hear it and do it," but his word is very nigh unto us in our hearts. This building conveys the sense of dignity and permanence befitting a house of religion. It has the feeling of reverence and seems to say, "The Lord is in his holy temple; let all the earth keep silence before him." It is informed by that spirit of beauty which led the Psalmist to say, "Worship the Lord in the beauty of holiness."

BOARD OF TRUSTEES 1905–6
T. J. Skillin, Chairman
W. G. Adams
W. A. Hutchinson
John Lewis
Herman Fietsch
R. F. Flinterman
Secretary, Guy Parke Conger, M. D.
Treasurer, James H. Heald, Jr.

BOARD OF TRUSTEES 1904–5
W. G. Adams, Chairman
John Lewis
E. H. Ehrman
Herman Fietsch
R. F. Flinterman
C. A. Sturtevant
Secretary, Guy Parke Conger, M. D.
Treasurer, James H. Heald, Jr.

SPECIAL COMMITTEES

ON SITE
James H. Heald
E. R. Haase
Chris Hafner

ON PLANS
R. F. Johonnot
E. H. Ehrman
Mrs. A. W. Bryant
Mrs. John Lewis
Jas. H. Heald, Jr.

ON WAYS AND MEANS
H. A. Taylor
W. S. Holden
C. A. Sharpe
D. G. Trench
Charles S. Woodard

ON BUILDING
E. H. Ehrman
Charles E. Roberts
C. A. Sharpe

COMMITTEE ON BROCHURE
Charles S. Woodard
R. F. Johonnot
Frank Lloyd Wright